the Jesus Storybook Bible

Every story whispers his name

Coloring Book

WORDS INSPIRED BY SALLY LLOYD-JONES • ILLUSTRATED BY JAGO

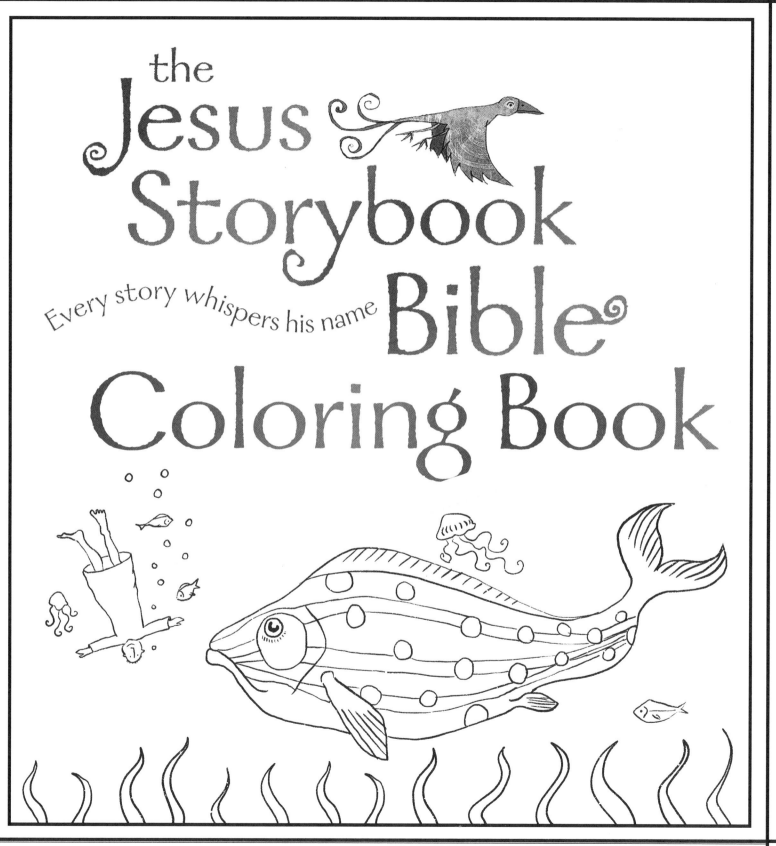

the
Jesus
Storybook
Every story whispers his name **Bible**
Coloring Book

ZONDERkidz

ZONDERKIDZ

The Jesus Storybook Bible Coloring Book
Copyright © 2020 by Sally Lloyd-Jones
Illustrations © 2020 by Jago

Requests for information should be addressed to:

Zonderkidz, 3900 Sparks Drive SE, Grand Rapids, Michigan 49546

Any internet addresses (websites, blogs, etc.) and telephone numbers in this book
are offered as a resource. They are not intended in any way to be or imply an
endorsement by Zondervan, nor does Zondervan vouch for the content of these
sites and numbers for the life of this book.

Zonderkidz is a trademark of Zondervan.

Interior design: Ron Huizinga

Printed in China

19 20 21 22 23 /DSC/ 10 9 8 7 6 5 4 3 2 1

God created everything in the world.

God made Adam and Eve and loved them with all of his heart.

The snake whispered a terrible lie to Eve.

God told Noah to build an ark.

God told Noah, "Bring all the animals aboard."

 All through the storm, God kept them safe.

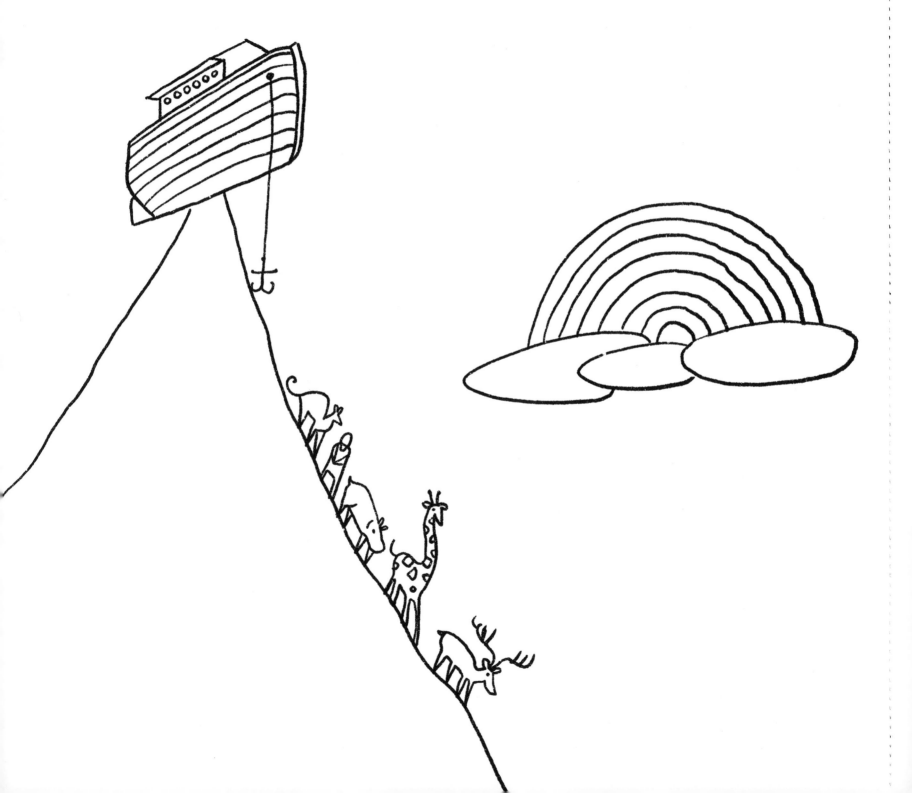

God promised Abraham more children than stars in the sky.

Just as God promised, Abraham and Sarah had a baby.

Joseph was Jacob's favorite son. Jacob made him a special coat.

God spoke to his friend Moses from a burning bush.

Pharaoh and all his chariots chased God's people.

God opened the way for them through the sea.

Jericho was a huge city with big, strong walls.

Joshua followed God's plan and the walls crumbled.

God's people wanted a king. They chose Saul.

 David didn't need armor or a sword—GOD would fight for him.

The giant was big. David was small. But God helped David win.

David was a shepherd and a songwriter too.

God promised Isaiah, "I am going to mend my broken world."

Daniel prayed only to God. So he was thrown into the lions' den.

But God sent an angel to save Daniel from the lions.

Jonah wanted to run away from God.

God sent a fish to rescue Jonah from the storm.

God forgave Jonah and gave him a second chance.

"Mary, you're going to have a baby boy. He is God's own Son!"

God's Son, Jesus, was born where the animals stayed—a stable.

God put a new star in the sky to shine right over the stable.

The angel said, "God's Son has been born! Go and see him!"

The shepherds found Mary and Joseph and the baby.

Three Wise Men followed the same star to find the baby king.

John the Baptist helped people get their hearts ready for Jesus.

A loud voice from heaven said, "This is my Son. Listen to him."

"Let's go!" Jesus said. And they dropped everything and went.

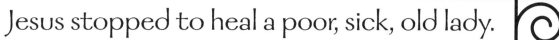 Jesus stopped to heal a poor, sick, old lady.

Jesus said, "God listens to you because he loves you."

Wherever Jesus went people went. He told them about God's love.

Jesus was tired and he fell asleep in the boat.

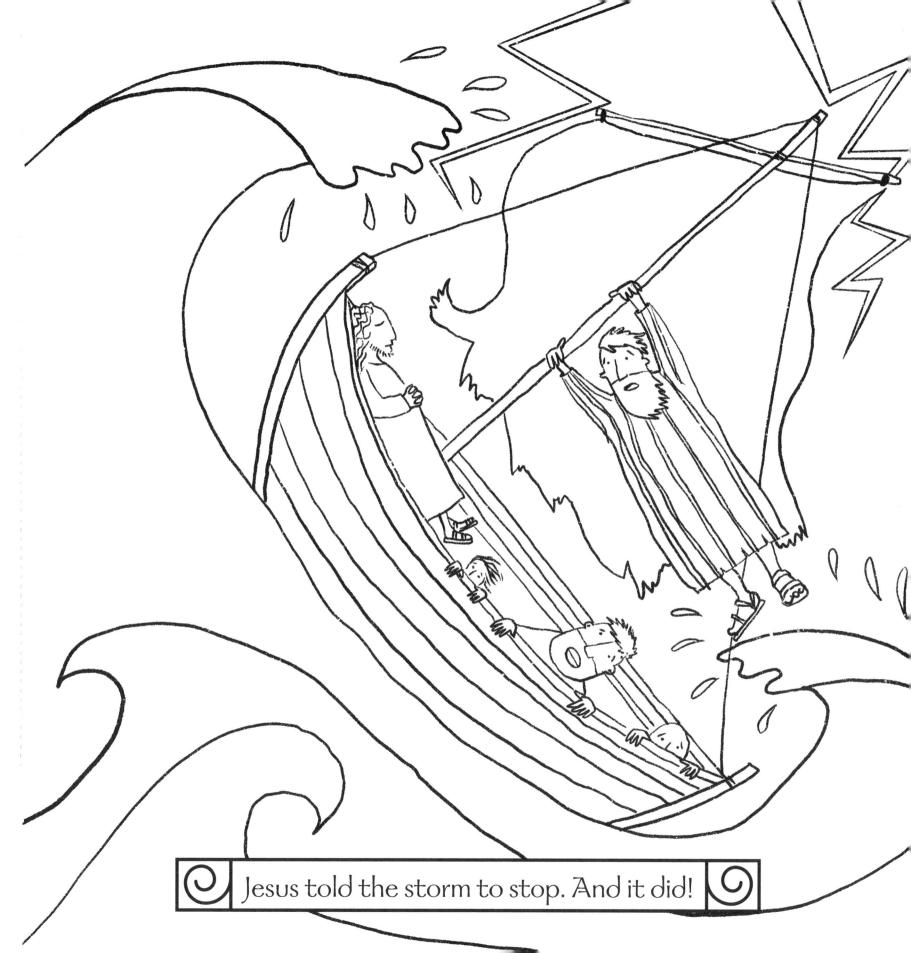

Jesus told the storm to stop. And it did!

The little boy gave Jesus everything he had.

Jesus told stories called parables to help people know God.

God's love is a gift. All you have to do is open your hands.

Zacchaeus saw Jesus and Jesus saw Zacchaeus.

Jesus loved Zacchaeus even when no one else did.

God is like a dad who won't ever stop loving his children.

Jesus knelt down to wash his friends' feet, like a lowly servant.

"Whenever you eat and drink, remember I have rescued you."

Jesus' friends were too tired to keep watch.

The soldiers came in the night and arrested Jesus.

They didn't realize Jesus had come to rescue them.

But it was God's plan to rescue the WHOLE WORLD.

An angel said, "Jesus is ALIVE again!"

"Mary!" Only one person said her name like that.

Jesus ate a whole fish. "Can a ghost do that?"

God sent help. He sent his spirit to fill their hearts with love.

Peter said, "Stop running away from God. He loves you!"

Saul hadn't met Jesus. So one day Jesus met Saul.

John had a beautiful dream about heaven.